Birds Take Flight

by Lillian Duggan

Scott Foresman
is an imprint of

PEARSON

Glenview, Illinois • Boston, Massachusetts • Chandler, Arizona
Upper Saddle River, New Jersey

ISBN 13: 978-0-328-51647-6
ISBN 10:   0-328-51647-3

3 4 5 6 7 8 9 10 V0N4 13 12 11 10

Mysterious Migration

Have you ever looked up into the sky and noticed a giant letter *V* soaring high above you? The V is probably made up of migrating birds, such as geese, ducks, and others. Migrating birds can be found throughout the world, from the Arctic Circle in the north to Antarctica in the south.

Migrating birds have their own unique migration behaviors, or habits. For example, they may **migrate** at different times of the year or in different patterns. Some even have special ways of getting to their destination.

For hundreds of years, scientists and others have been curious about the migration habits of birds. Why do birds migrate? Where do they go? Is there a reason some birds fly in a V formation when they migrate? How do they navigate?

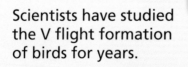

Scientists have studied the V flight formation of birds for years.

Why Birds Migrate

Birds generally migrate when the seasons begin to change. When cold winter weather arrives, many birds that spend the spring in the north travel south. Later, when warmer spring weather returns, these birds head back north again.

People often think that birds leave places that become cold because they cannot survive freezing temperatures, but this is not actually the case. Warmer places have more sunlight and plants, which means there are more insects and fruit–the birds' food.

Hummingbird

Birds return home once the trees and flowers bloom again in the spring. Spring is a great time of year for birds to find food for their young as well as gather materials for nest building. In the spring the birds return home to breed, lay eggs, and nest.

Many species of hummingbirds are migratory. They migrate from the northern United States and Canada to Mexico or Central America. Hummingbirds return north each spring when the flowers that provide their food bloom.

This mother hummingbird is feeding her young. Hummingbirds breed sometime between March and August.

Migration Routes

When North American birds migrate, they follow four general routes, known as **flyways.** These are the Atlantic flyway, the Pacific flyway, the Mississippi flyway, and the Central flyway.

Birds travel along these four flyways for several reasons. First, the flyways follow major land formations, such as the Atlantic and Pacific coasts, the Mississippi River valley, and the Sierra Nevada and Rocky and Appalachian Mountains. Each of these land formations lies in a north-to-south direction, so birds can follow the formations and use them as a guide.

Another reason birds travel along flyways is the same as their motivation to migrate—food. Coastal areas offer an abundant supply of food for migrating shorebirds, and birds traveling inland can find plenty to eat along the Mississippi River valley.

Finally, some birds can travel faster by flying over mountains. Above mountain ranges, warm air moves upward over the high slopes, and this movement of air creates rising air currents called **thermals.** Birds, such as eagles, vultures, and hawks, use thermals to help them save energy when they are flying.

North American Migration Flyways

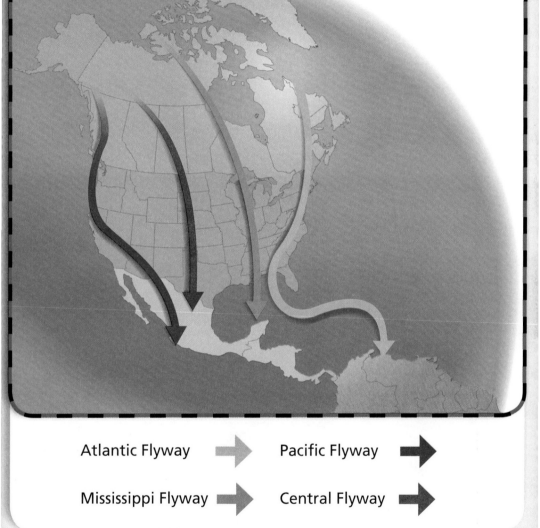

Atlantic Flyway ➡   Pacific Flyway ➡

Mississippi Flyway ➡   Central Flyway ➡

How Birds Navigate

As you've read, North American birds tend to follow the four flyways when they migrate. In fact, people have observed birds slowing down in flight to search for landmarks, such as river valleys and hills. Birds use these landmarks to figure out where they are. Most birds, however, do not follow land formations the entire time they are in the air. Birds have other ways of **navigating**, or finding their way when in flight.

Birds use the position of the sun and the stars to determine where they are going. Some birds that migrate at night use the location of the setting sun to get them started. An experiment showed how night-migrating birds inside a planetarium figured out where they were by following the pattern of stars glowing on the ceiling.

Birds are able to find their way, even at night.

Birds also have extraordinary senses of sight and hearing that help them figure out where they are as they fly. They can see ultraviolet light emitted from the sun, and they can hear the sound of ocean waves and wind blowing over mountains thousands of miles away. Birds use their senses, along with their keen sense of the environment, to reach their destination. These navigators continue to get where they need to go, and many live to do so year, after year, after year.

Scientists studying European robins learned that birds may be able to see Earth's magnetic field.

Flocks

Different species of birds make the long journey between their winter and summer homes in different ways. For example, some species travel alone, and others travel in groups. A group of birds traveling together is called a **flock,** and a single flock might be made up of hundreds of birds.

You have probably seen flocks of birds flying above your neighborhood. Some flocks fly in an unorganized group, while others move in a pattern, or formation.

The three types of formations are clusters, lines, and compound, or combination, lines. Cluster formations are the most common, and some birds form flat clusters, while others fly in vertical stacks.

Line formations are the simplest, which are how some ducks fly–in long straight lines. Other birds form compound line formations when they combine lines to form shapes, such as a J, U, or V.

These birds fly as a flock.

Flocks in a V Formation

Many birds, including geese, pelicans, and cranes, fly in a V formation. For years, scientists have tried to learn why these birds fly in this manner. Many believed that the birds saved energy this way, but they were unable to prove their theory, or educated guess.

In 2001 a team of French scientists developed a way to test this theory on pelicans. They attached heart-rate monitors to a group of pelicans, and then the scientists measured the pelicans' heart rates when they flew solo and when they flew in a V. After the scientists collected their data, they compared the heart rates.

The scientists learned that the birds' heart rates were higher when they flew solo than when they flew in formation. The higher a bird's heart rate, the more energy the bird uses. So the French scientists' hunch was correct—pelicans do use less energy when they fly in a V formation!

These pelicans are flying in a V formation. Scientists studying pelicans solved the mystery of the V.

Saving Energy

Why did the pelicans in the study save energy when they flew in a V formation? The answer, the scientists found, is that the pelicans could glide more often when flying with a group. Gliding requires little energy because the birds don't have to flap their wings.

A bird flying in a V formation can glide part of the time because the bird in front of it creates a **vortex** when it flaps its wings. A vortex is a mass of air that moves in a circular motion. Inside the circle of moving air is an empty space called a vacuum, which has a force that pulls objects toward it. That force helps the bird, which is flying behind, to move along, allowing it to glide for a period of time.

Many examples of vortexes can be found in nature, but perhaps the most familiar one is a tornado. A tornado is a funnel-shaped cloud that spins violently, creating whirling winds that are powerful enough to destroy buildings and uproot trees.

When birds fly in a V formation, they save a great deal of energy. They can use this energy to travel farther during migration.

This diagram shows how a bird's wing beat creates a vortex that makes flying easier for birds behind it in a V formation.

This bird's wing beat pushes air down.

The vortex pulls this bird forward so it can glide.

Nearby air pushes up, creating a vortex.

North American V Flyers

The pelicans studied by the French scientists were great white pelicans. These pelicans live in Europe, Asia, and Africa. Many other bird species that fly in a V formation live in North America. These include Canada and snow geese, double-crested cormorants, canvasback ducks, and whooping cranes.

Geese

The honk that you may hear high above your head in the springtime is likely to be a flock of Canada geese flying in a V formation.

Canada geese live all over the United States and in most of Canada. Some migrate from northern Canada and Alaska to the southern United States and Mexico. Some Canada geese begin migrating back north in January or February, but others wait until March to begin their journey.

Canada geese live anywhere near water. You may have seen some where you live since they can be found in city parks, on golf courses, and near rivers and lakes.

Snow geese also fly in a V formation. Snow geese spend their winters in the southern United States and Mexico, but in June, they fly thousands of miles north to the Arctic tundra of northern Canada.

For most of the year, the Arctic tundra is frozen and nearly lifeless, so very few animal species live there year-round. This makes the tundra an ideal place for snow geese to breed because they have little competition for food. In the spring, when the tundra thaws and comes back to life, snow geese flock there by the thousands.

Snow geese nest in large groups. As many as twelve hundred nests can be found in one square mile.

Double-crested Cormorant

Another North American bird that flies in a V formation is the double-crested cormorant. This bird spends the winter in the southern United States and the summer on the northern Pacific and Atlantic coasts. Double-crested cormorants live in lakes, rivers, swamps, and along coastlines.

Some double-crested cormorants do not migrate. Instead, they live year-round along the Pacific coast and in Alaska.

A double-crested cormorant looks similar to a duck, but it is actually a close relative of the pelican.

Watching double-crested cormorants eat is entertaining because of the way these birds dive underwater to catch a fish, return to the surface, flip the fish in the air, and swallow it head first.

The double-crested cormorant does not have waterproof feathers. It dries its wings by spreading them out.

Canvasback Duck

Canvasback ducks are known for being fast and high fliers. They often travel in a V formation, but sometimes they travel in a line.

Canvasbacks normally breed in western Canada and the northwestern United States in summertime. They build their nests in the shallow marshes of prairie regions. Occasionally, a major drought in the northern Great Plains of the United States will force them to move farther north, and some migrate as far as Alaska.

In winter, the ducks head to Mexico and the Atlantic and Gulf coasts of the United States, where they live mostly in saltwater bays.

Similar to double-crested cormorants, canvasbacks dive for their food. They eat the roots of underwater plants, as well as some small animals.

Large flocks of canvasback ducks can be found along the Mississippi River and in Chesapeake Bay by the middle of November.

Whooping Cranes

Whooping cranes live in North America. With their necks stretched out in front, cranes fly long distances when they migrate.

Like eagles, vultures, and hawks, cranes will sometimes coast along thermals. But, before they take flight, cranes need to get a running start along the ground.

Whooping cranes live in grassy wetland areas. They spend the spring in the northern United States and Canada, and they winter between the southern United States and Central America.

The migratory range of whooping cranes is quite small because the whooping crane population is also very small, though **conservationists** are trying to help protect them. Whooping cranes are an **endangered species.** Endangered species are animals that are in danger of becoming extinct, or no longer existing. In 1850 the total whooping crane population in North America was fifteen hundred birds, but by 1941 it had dropped to just sixteen birds.

Conservationists are people who try to preserve and protect natural resources. In the past, to help prevent the extinction of the whooping crane, conservationists made efforts to change these birds' migration routes so that they would breed in healthy environments. That effort failed, but overall, conservationists have been successful because, by late 2003, the whooping crane population reached 426 birds.

Whooping cranes perform an exciting dance when they find a mate. They flap their wings, bob up and down, and leap into the air.

Airplanes in a V Formation

For many centuries, humans have tried to join birds and take to the skies. Beginning with inventor Leonardo da Vinci in the fifteenth century, on to the Wright brothers in the nineteenth century, many people have studied the flight of birds.

Scientists today are still studying bird flight in hopes of improving the performance of airplanes. At the National Aeronautics and Space Administration (NASA), scientists have been trying to mimic birds by flying airplanes in a V formation. NASA has flown several test flights with two fighter jets, where one jet flies in the vortex of the other.

NASA scientists think that airplanes can save energy the same way geese and other birds do. When airplanes save energy, they use less fuel. This is helpful because not only is fuel expensive, but burning it is hazardous to the environment as well.

NASA's project has had great results because airplanes flying in a V formation have reduced their fuel usage by up to 30 percent. If passenger planes could fly this way, airlines could save millions of dollars in fuel costs, and planes would release less pollution into the environment.

NASA hopes that one day passenger airplanes will fly as a group in a formation similar to birds. Then air traffic controllers will be able to manage these planes as if they were a single plane.

Perhaps someday people will travel the same way that geese, double-crested cormorants, canvasback ducks, and whooping cranes do. These birds follow the flyways in search of the right spot to bring their young into the world. And they do this in such a fascinating way!

These two jets are performing test flights for NASA. The plane in back is flying in the vortex made by the plane in front.

Water Vortex

When birds flap their wings, they create a vortex of air. Another air vortex you may have seen (hopefully, not in person) is a tornado. A vortex can also be made from liquid. Think about the funnel of water that whirls down your bathtub drain when you unplug it. That's a liquid vortex.

What You Will Need

Ask an adult to help you find these things:
- two empty one-liter soda bottles with labels removed
- a rubber or steel washer that is the same width as the tops of the bottles
- a roll of duct tape
- water

1. Fill one bottle three-quarters full of water.

2. Using the duct tape, tape the washer to the top of the bottle filled with water. Make sure you don't tape over the hole in the washer.

3. Place the empty bottle upside down on top of the washer. Tape the two bottles together.

4. Turn the bottles over so the one with the water is on top. Quickly swirl the bottles in a circular motion a few times, then place the bottom bottle on a table. Watch the water closely. What does it look like?

5. Think about the kind of vortex that birds make when they flap their wings. How do you think this water vortex is similar to that kind? How do you think it's different?

Glossary

conservationists *n.* people who try to preserve and protect natural resources.

endangered species *n.* an animal that is in danger of becoming extinct.

flock *n.* a group of birds traveling together.

flyways *n.* routes traveled often by migratory birds.

migrate *v.* to go from one region to another with the change in the seasons.

navigating *v.* moving to find a position or place.

thermals *n.* rising currents of air.

vortex *n.* a mass of air that moves in a circular motion and surrounds a vacuum.